Greetings human, and welcome to the first volume of *SCARECROWOVEN'S GLORG WORSHIP*, a brief anthology of both commercial and fine art works by Scarecrowoven. Here, you will find terrible maggots of mayhem, the beheading of the behemoth of Lando-Lando Land, spittoon fever, ancient spirits from the cave of lost souls, Fantasy ice skating murder, the soul spear of Genghis Khan, Yugla the Glorg, shrieking space eels, and severed Yeti fingers. All images have mystical incantations encrypted within, so take caution. If this book begins to speak, hiss or emit light from unknown source, bury book 3 feet deep in soil 3 miles away from home. Discontinue use of book if any of the flowing occurs: dizziness, burning, vulgar itchiness, oozing sore or boners, vomiting, or grotesque sex fantasies. This moment shall never be again, so bite down hard, we are connected.

- *www.scarecrowoven.com* • *www.scarecrowoven.bigcartel.com* -

Fright-Rags | pencil, colored pencil, airbrush and ink
on bristol board with additional digital colors

HorrorHound Records | ink on bristol board, Digital colors

LUSTRATION

HARLEY POE LEVEL IV

ink on bristol board,
Digital colors

HorrorHound
Records

HorrorHound Records | ink on bristol board, Digital colors

ink on bristol board.
Digital colors | **HorrorHound Records**

HorrorHound Records | ink on bristol board, Digital colors

LUSTRATION

HARLEY POE LEVEL I

ink on bristol board.
Digital colors

HorrorHound
Records

Fright-Rags | pencil, airbrush and ink
on bristol board with digital colors

Fright-Rags | airbrush and ink
on bristol board with digital colors

Headless
horseman records | ink on bristol board with digital colors

Fright-Rags | airbrush and ink
on bristol board with digital colors

WOLF ANCESTOR DEFENSE

ink on bristol board
digital colors

**Bottleneck
Gallery**

Glitch Gallery | acrylic paint and india ink on illustration board.

ink on bristol board | **Landyachtz**
digital colors | **Skateboards**

Friday Night | pencil, colored pencil and ink
Lights | on bristol board with digital colors

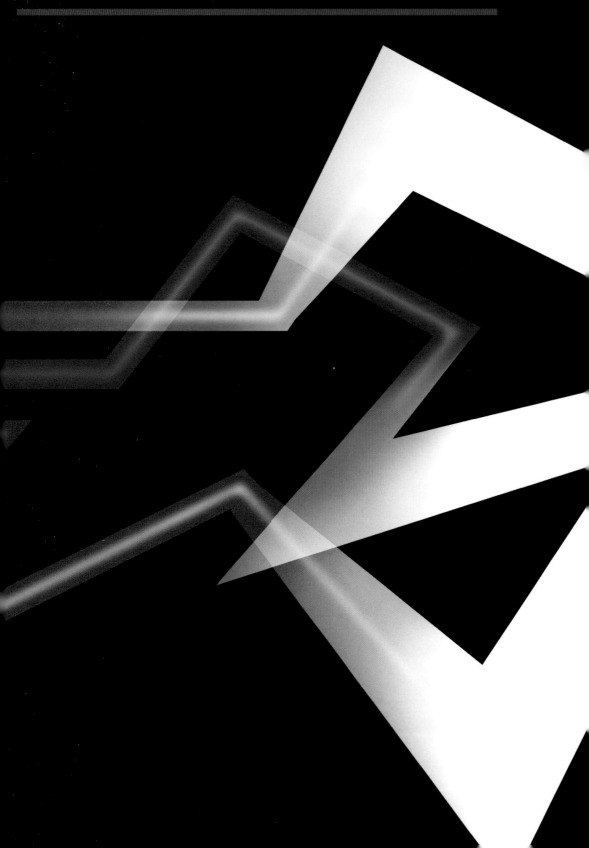

Fright-Rags | pencil, colored pencil, airbrush and ink
on bristol board with digital colors

pencil and airbrush
on bristol board | **Fright-Rags**

Dread Central | pencil, colored pencil, airbrush and ink on bristol board with digital colors

pencil, colored pencil, airbrush and ink | Fright-Rags
on bristol board with digital colors

**Ernie Ball
Guitar Strings** | ink on bristol board with digital colors

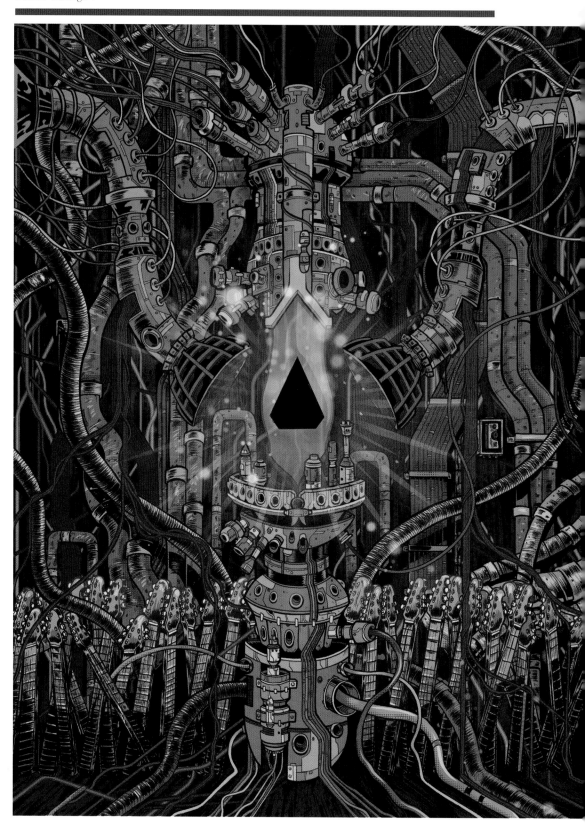

Creature Skateboards | ink on bristol board with digital colors

Creature
Skateboards | ink on bristol board
with digital colors

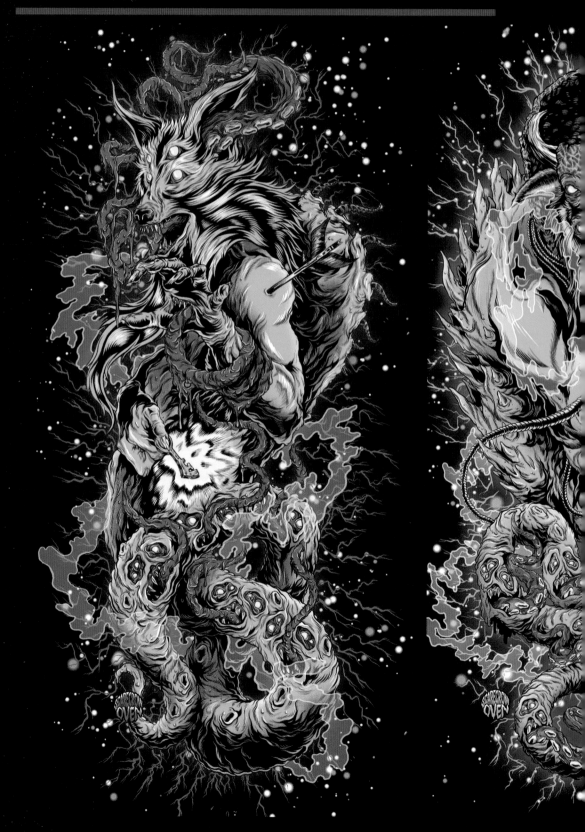

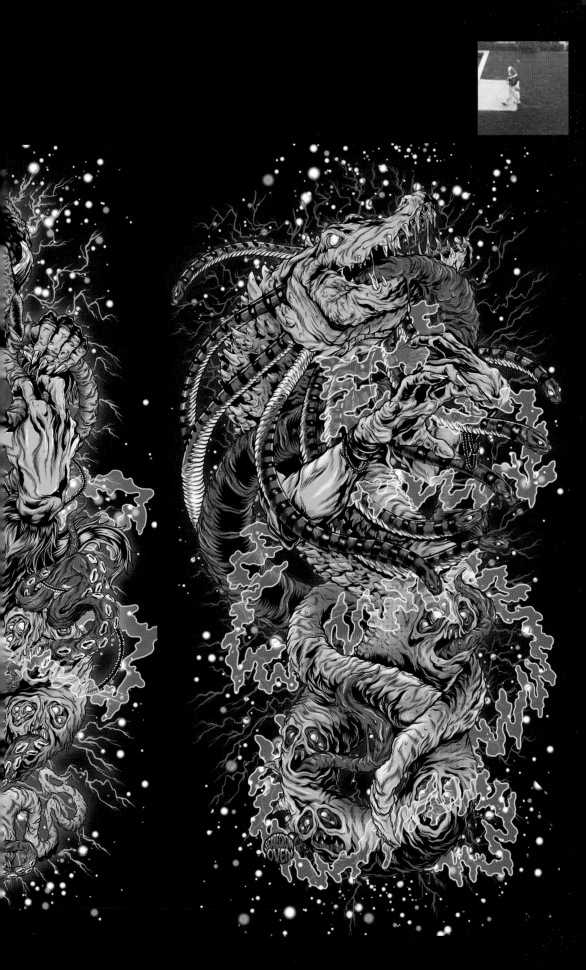

Landyachtz Skateboards | ink on bristol board with digital colors

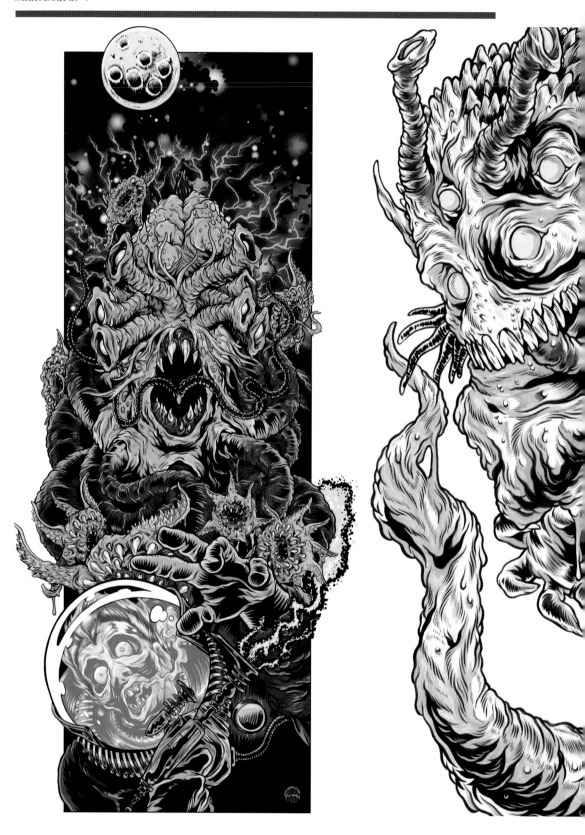

acrylic and ink on illustration board | Glitch
                                              Gallery

HorrorHound| airbrush and ink
Radio | on bristol board with digital colors

ink on bristol board with digital colors | I Dream in Plastic

Expanded | pencil, colored pencil, airbrush and ink
Universe | on bristol board with additional digital colors

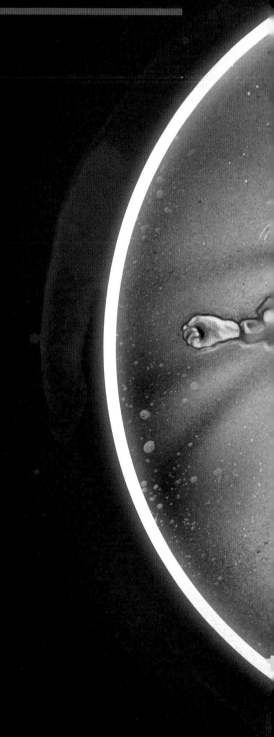

**Style Over
Substance** | ink on bristol board with digital colors

ink on bristol board | **Andrew**
digital colors | **Maclean**

Ministry | ink on bristol board with digital colors

HorrorHound
Magazine

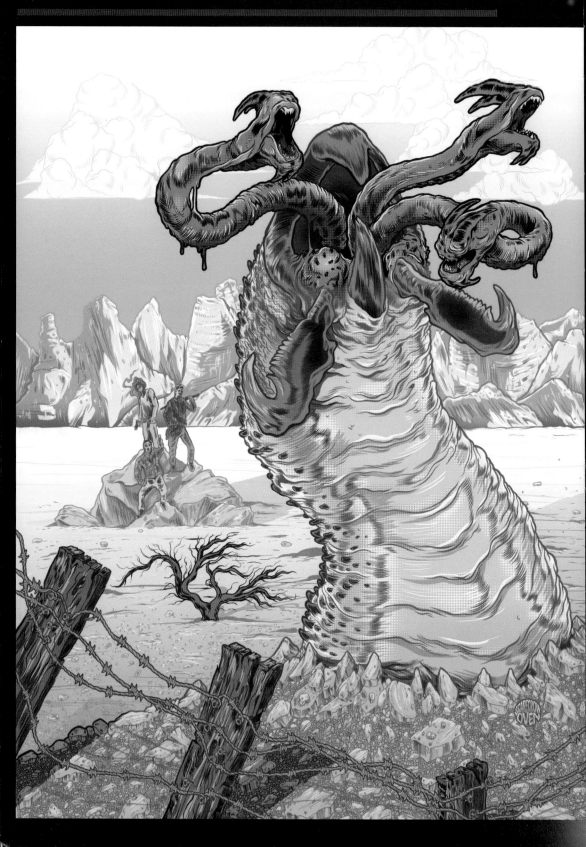

pencil and airbrush on bristol board
with additional digital color

Xavier, Kerrie and Milo